CONGREGATION FOR THE DOCTRINE OF THE FAITH

LETTER

SAMARITANUS BONUS

ON THE CARE OF PERSONS IN THE CRITICAL AND TERMINAL PHASES OF LIFE

*All documents are published
thanks to the generosity of the supporters
of the Catholic Truth Society*

Cover image: Pelegrí Clavé i Roquer, The Good Samaritan (1838), inv. 00217.
Reial Acadèmia Catalana de Belles Arts de Sant Jordi.

This edition first published 2020 by The Incorporated Catholic Truth Society
42-46 Harleyford Road London SE11 5AY.

Libreria Editrice Vaticana omnia sibi vindicat iura. Sine eiusdem licentia
scripto data nemini liceat hunc Samaritanum Bonum denuo imprimere aut in
aliam linguam vertere. Copyright © 2020 Libreria Editrice Vaticana 00120
Città del Vaticano. Tel. 06.698.45780 – Fax 06.698.84716 Email: commerciale.
lev@spc.va

ISBN 978 1 78469 646 7

CONTENTS

INTRODUCTION

The Good Samaritan who goes out of his way to aid an injured man (cf. *Lk* 10:30-37) signifies Jesus Christ who encounters man in need of salvation and cares for his wounds and suffering with "the oil of consolation and the wine of hope".[1] He is the physician of souls and bodies, "the faithful witness" (*Rev* 3:14) of the divine salvific presence in the world. How to make this message concrete today? How to translate it into a readiness to accompany a suffering person in the terminal stages of life in this world, and to offer this assistance in a way that respects and promotes the intrinsic human dignity of persons who are ill, their vocation to holiness, and thus the highest worth of their existence?

The remarkable progressive development of biomedical technologies has exponentially enlarged the clinical proficiency of diagnostic medicine in patient care and treatment. The Church regards scientific research and technology with hope, seeing in them promising opportunities to serve the integral good of life and the dignity of every human being.[2] Nonetheless, advances in medical technology, though precious, cannot in themselves define the proper meaning and value of human life. In fact, every technical advance in healthcare calls for growth in moral discernment[3] to avoid an unbalanced and dehumanising use of the technologies especially in the critical or terminal stages of human life.

---

[1] Roman Missal (Italian Edition), renewed by decree of the Second Ecumenical Council of the Vatican, promulgated by authority of Pope Paul VI and revised at the direction of Pope John Paul II. Italian Episcopal Conference - Fondazione di Religione Santi Francesco d'Assisi e Caterina da Siena, Rome 2020, Common Preface VIII. p. 404.

[2] Cf. Pontifical Council for Pastoral Assistance to Health Care Workers, *New Charter for Health Care Workers*, National Catholic Bioethics Center, Philadelphia, PA, 2017, n. 6.

[3] Cf. Benedict XVI, Encyclical Letter *Spe salvi* (30th November 2007), 22: *AAS* 99 (2007), 1004. "If technical progress is not matched by corresponding progress in man's ethical formation, in man's inner growth (cf. *Eph* 3:16; *2 Cor* 4:16), then it is not progress at all, but a threat for man and for the world".

Moreover, the organisational management and sophistication, as well as the complexity of contemporary healthcare delivery, can reduce to a purely technical and impersonal relationship the bond of trust between physician and patient. This danger arises particularly where governments have enacted legislation to legalise forms of assisted suicide and voluntary euthanasia among the most vulnerable of the sick and infirm. The ethical and legal boundaries that protect the self-determination of the sick person are transgressed by such legislation, and, to a worrying degree, the value of human life during times of illness, the meaning of suffering, and the significance of the interval preceding death are eclipsed. Pain and death do not constitute the ultimate measures of the human dignity that is proper to every person by the very fact that they are "human beings".

In the face of challenges that affect the very way we think about medicine, the significance of the care of the sick, and our social responsibility toward the most vulnerable, the present letter seeks to enlighten pastors and the faithful regarding their questions and uncertainties about medical care, and their spiritual and pastoral obligations to the sick in the critical and terminal stages of life. All are called to give witness at the side of the sick person and to become a "healing community" in order to actualise concretely the desire of Jesus that, beginning with the most weak and vulnerable, all may be one flesh.[4] It is widely recognised that a moral and practical clarification regarding care of these persons is needed. In this sensitive area comprising the most delicate and decisive stages of a person's life, a "unity of teaching and practice is certainly necessary."[5]

Various Episcopal Conferences around the world have published pastoral letters and statements to address the challenges posed to healthcare professionals and patients

---

[4] Cf. Francis, *Speech to the Italian Association against Leukemia, Lymphoma and Myeloma (AIL)* (2nd March 2019): *L'Osservatore Romano*, 3rd March 2019, 7.

[5] Francis, Apostolic Exhortation *Amoris laetitia* (19th March 2016), 3: *AAS* 108 (2016), 312.

especially in Catholic institutions by the legalisation of assisted suicide and voluntary euthanasia in some countries. Regarding the celebration of the Sacraments for those who intend to bring an end to their own life, the provision of spiritual assistance in particular situations raises questions that today require a more clear and precise intervention on the part of the Church in order to:

- reaffirm the message of the Gospel and its expression in the basic doctrinal statements of the Magisterium, and thus to recall the mission of all who come into contact with the sick at critical and terminal stages (relatives or legal guardians, hospital chaplains, extraordinary ministers of the Eucharist and pastoral workers, hospital volunteers and healthcare personnel), as well as the sick themselves; and,

- provide precise and concrete pastoral guidelines to deal with these complex situations at the local level and to handle them in a way that fosters the patient's personal encounter with the merciful love of God.

I. CARE FOR ONE'S NEIGHBOUR

Despite our best efforts, it is hard to recognise the profound value of human life when we see it in its weakness and fragility. Far from being outside the existential horizon of the person, suffering always raises limitless questions about the meaning of life.[6] These pressing questions cannot be answered solely by human reflection, because in suffering there is concealed *the immensity of a specific mystery* that can only be disclosed by the Revelation of God.[7] In particular, the mission of faithful care of human life until its natural conclusion[8] is entrusted to every healthcare worker and is realised through programmes of care that can restore, even in illness and suffering, a deep awareness of their existence to every patient. For this reason, we begin with a careful consideration of the significance of the specific mission entrusted by God to every person, healthcare professional and pastoral worker, as well as to patients and their families.

The need for medical care is born in the vulnerability of the human condition in its finitude and limitations. Each person's vulnerability is encoded in our nature as a unity of body and soul: we are materially and temporally finite, and yet we have a longing for the infinite and a destiny that is eternal. As creatures who are by nature finite, yet nonetheless destined for eternity, we depend on material goods and on the mutual support of other persons, and also on our original, deep connection with God. Our vulnerability forms the basis for an *ethics of care*, especially in the medical field, which is expressed in concern, dedication, shared participation and responsibility towards

---

[6] Cf. Second Vatican Ecumenical Council, Pastoral Constitution *Gaudium et spes*, 10: *AAS* 58 (1966), 1032-1033.

[7] Cf. John Paul II, Apostolic Letter *Salvifici doloris* (11th February 1984), 4: *AAS* 76 (1984), 203.

[8] Cf. Pontifical Council for Pastoral Assistance to Healthcare Workers, *New Charter for Healthcare Workers*, n. 144.

the women and men entrusted to us for material and spiritual assistance in their hour of need.

The relationship of care discloses the twofold dimension of the principle of justice: to promote human life (*suum cuique tribuere*) and to avoid harming another (*alterum non laedere*). Jesus transformed this principle into the golden rule "Do unto others whatever you would have them do to you" (*Mt* 7:12). This rule is echoed in the maxim *primum non nocere* of traditional medical ethics.

Care for life is therefore the first responsibility that guides the physician in the encounter with the sick. Since its anthropological and moral horizon is broader, this responsibility exists not only when the restoration to health is a realistic outcome, but even when a cure is unlikely or impossible. Medical and nursing care necessarily attends to the body's physiological functions, as well as to the psychological and spiritual well-being of the patient who should never be forsaken. Along with the many sciences upon which it draws, medicine also possesses the key dimension of a "therapeutic art," entailing robust relationships with the patient, with healthcare workers, with relatives, and with members of communities to which the patient is linked. *Therapeutic art, clinical procedures* and *ongoing care* are inseparably interwoven in the practice of medicine, especially at the critical and terminal stages of life.

The Good Samaritan, in fact, "not only draws nearer to the man he finds half dead; he takes responsibility for him".[9] He invests in him, not only with the funds he has on hand but also with funds he does not have and hopes to earn in Jericho: he promises to pay any additional costs upon his return. Likewise, Christ invites us to trust in his invisible grace that prompts us to the generosity of supernatural charity, as we identify with everyone who is ill: "Amen, I say to you, whatever you did for one of

---

[9] Francis, *Message for the 48th World Communications Day* (1st June 2014): *AAS* 106 (2014), 114.

these least brothers of mine, you did for me" (*Mt* 25:40). This affirmation expresses a moral truth of universal scope: "we need then to *'show care'* for all life and for the life of everyone"[10] and thus to reveal the original and unconditional love of God, the source of the meaning of all life.

To that end, especially in hospitals and clinics committed to Christian values, it is vital to create space for relationships built on the recognition of the *fragility* and *vulnerability* of the sick person. Weakness makes us conscious of our dependence on God and invites us to respond with the respect due to our neighbour. Every individual who cares for the sick (physician, nurse, relative, volunteer, pastor) has the moral responsibility to apprehend the fundamental and inalienable good that is the human person. They should adhere to the highest standards of self-respect and respect for others by embracing, safeguarding and promoting human life until natural death. At work here is a *contemplative gaze*[11] that beholds in one's own existence and that of others a unique and unrepeatable wonder, received and welcomed as a gift. This is the gaze of the one who does not pretend to take possession of the reality of life but welcomes it as it is, with its difficulties and sufferings, and, guided by faith, finds in illness the readiness to abandon oneself to the Lord of life who is manifest therein.

To be sure, medicine must accept the limit of death as part of the human condition. The time comes when it is clear that specific medical interventions cannot alter the course of an illness that is recognised to be terminal. It is a dramatic reality, that must be communicated to the sick person both with great humanity and with openness in faith to a supernatural horizon, aware of the anguish that death involves especially in a culture that tries to conceal it. One cannot think of physical life as something to

---

[10] John Paul II, Encyclical Letter *Evangelium vitae* (25th March 1995), 87: *AAS* 87 (1995), 500.

[11] Cf. John Paul II, Encyclical Letter *Centesimus annus* (1st May 1991), 37: *AAS* 83 (1991), 840.

preserve at all costs – which is impossible – but as something to live in the free acceptance of the meaning of bodily existence: "only in reference to the human person in his 'unified totality', that is as 'a soul which expresses itself in a body and a body informed by an immortal spirit', can the specifically human meaning of the body be grasped".[12]

The impossibility of a cure where death is imminent does not entail the cessation of medical and nursing activity. Responsible communication with the terminally ill person should make it clear that care will be provided until the very end: *"to cure if possible, always to care"*.[13] The obligation always to take care of the sick provides criteria to assess the actions to be undertaken in an "incurable" illness: the judgement that an illness is incurable cannot mean that care has come at an end. The contemplative gaze calls for a wider notion of care. The objective of assistance must take account of the integrity of the person, and thus deploy adequate measures to provide the necessary physical, psychological, social, familial and religious support to the sick. The living faith of the persons involved in care contributes to the authentic theologal life of the sick person, even if this is not immediately evident. The pastoral care of all - family, doctors, nurses, and chaplains - can help the patient to persevere in sanctifying grace and to die in charity and the Love of God. Where faith is absent in the face of the inevitability of illness, especially when chronic or degenerative, fear of suffering, death, and the discomfort they entail is the main factor driving the attempt to control and manage the moment of death, and indeed to hasten it through euthanasia or assisted suicide.

---

[12] John Paul II, Encyclical Letter *Veritatis splendor* (6th August 1993), 50: *AAS* 85 (1993), 1173.

[13] John Paul II, *Address to the participants in the International Congress "Life sustaining treatments and vegetative state. Scientific progress and ethical dilemmas"* (20th March 2004), 7: *AAS* 96 (2004), 489.

II. THE LIVING EXPERIENCE OF THE SUFFERING CHRIST AND THE PROCLAMATION OF HOPE

If the figure of the Good Samaritan throws new light on the provision of healthcare, the nearness of the God made man is manifest in the living experience of Christ's suffering, of his agony on the Cross and his Resurrection: his experience of multiple forms of pain and anguish resonates with the sick and their families during the long days of infirmity that precede the end of life.

Not only do the words of the prophet Isaiah proclaim Christ as one familiar with suffering and pain (cf. *Is* 53), but, as we re-read the pages about his suffering, we also recognise the experience of incredulity and scorn, abandonment, and physical pain and anguish. Christ's experience resonates with the sick who are often seen as a burden to society; their questions are not understood; they often undergo forms of affective desertion and the loss of connection with others.

Every sick person has the need not only to be heard, but to understand that their interlocutor "knows" what it means to feel alone, neglected, and tormented by the prospect of physical pain. Added to this is the suffering caused when society equates their value as persons to their quality of life and makes them feel like a burden to others. In this situation, to turn one's gaze to Christ is to turn to him who experienced in his flesh the pain of the lashes and nails, the derision of those who scourged him, and the abandonment and the betrayal of those closest to him.

In the face of the challenge of illness and the emotional and spiritual difficulties associated with pain, one must necessarily know how to speak a word of comfort drawn from the compassion of Jesus on the Cross. It is full of hope - a sincere hope, like Christ's on the Cross, capable of facing the moment of trial and the challenge of death. *Ave crux, spes unica*, we sing in the Good Friday liturgy. In the Cross of Christ are concentrated and recapitulated all the sickness and suffering of the world: all the *physical suffering*, of which the Cross, that instrument of an infamous and shameful death, is the symbol; all the *psychological suffering*, expressed in the death of Jesus in the darkest of solitude, abandonment and betrayal; all the *moral suffering*, manifested in the condemnation to death of one who is innocent; all the *spiritual suffering*, displayed in a desolation that seems like the very silence of God.

Christ is aware of the painful shock of his Mother and his disciples who "remain" under the Cross and who, though "remaining", appear impotent and resigned, and yet provide the affective intimacy that allows the God made man to live through hours that seem meaningless.

Then there is the Cross: an instrument of torture and execution reserved only for the lowest, that symbolically looks just like those afflictions that nail us to a bed, that portend only death, and that render meaningless time and its flow. Still, those who "remain" near the sick not only betoken but also embody affections, connections, along with a profound readiness to love. In all this, the suffering person can discern the human gaze that lends meaning to the time of illness. For, in the experience of being loved, all of life finds its justification. During his passion Christ was always sustained by his confident trust in the Father's love, so evident in the hours of the Cross, and also in his Mother's love. The Love of God always makes itself known in the history of men and women, thanks to the love of the one who never deserts us, who "remains," despite everything, at our side.

At the end of life, people often harbour worries about those they leave behind: about their children, spouses, parents, and friends. This human element can never be neglected and requires a sympathetic response.

14

With the same concern, Christ before his death thinks of his Mother who will remain alone within a sorrow that she will have to bear from now on. In the spare account of the Gospel of John, Christ turns to his Mother to reassure her and to entrust her to the care of the beloved disciple: "Woman, behold your son" (cf. *Jn* 19: 26-27). The end of life is a time of relationships, a time when loneliness and abandonment must be defeated (cf. *Mt* 27:46 and *Mk* 15:34) in the confident offering of one's life to God (cf. *Lk* 23:46).

In this perspective, to gaze at the crucifix is to behold a choral scene, where Christ is at the centre because he recapitulates in his own flesh and truly transfigures the darkest hours of the human experience, those in which he silently faces the possibility of despair. The light of faith enables us to discern the trinitarian presence in the brief, supple description provided by the Gospels, because Christ trusts in the Father thanks to the Holy Spirit who sustains his Mother and his disciples. In this way "they remain" and in their "remaining" at the foot of the Cross, they participate, with their human dedication to the Suffering One, in the mystery of Redemption.

In this manner, although marked by a painful passing, death can become the occasion of a greater hope that, thanks to faith, makes us participants in the redeeming work of Christ. Pain is existentially bearable only where there is hope. The hope that Christ communicates to the sick and the suffering is that of his presence, of his true nearness. Hope is not only the expectation of a greater good, but is a gaze on the present full of significance. In the Christian faith, the event of the Resurrection not only reveals eternal life, but it makes manifest that *in* history the last word never belongs to death, pain, betrayal, and suffering. Christ rises *in* history, and in the mystery of the Resurrection the abiding love of the Father is confirmed.

To contemplate the living experience of Christ's suffering is to proclaim to men and women of today a hope that imparts meaning to the time of sickness and death. From this hope springs the love that overcomes the temptation to despair.

While essential and invaluable, palliative care in itself is not enough unless there is someone who "remains" at the bedside of the sick to bear witness to their unique and unrepeatable value. For the believer, to look upon the Crucified means to trust in the compassionate love of God. In a time when autonomy and individualism are acclaimed, it must be remembered that, while it is true that everyone lives their own suffering, their own pain and their own death, these experiences always transpire in the presence of others and under their gaze. Nearby the Cross there are also the functionaries of the Roman state, there are the curious, there are the distracted, there are the indifferent and the resentful: they are at the Cross, but they do not "remain" with the Crucified.

In intensive care units or centres for chronic illness care, one can be present merely as a functionary, or as someone who "remains" with the sick.

The experience of the Cross enables us to be present to the suffering person as a genuine interlocutor with whom to speak a word or express a thought, or entrust the anguish and fear one feels. To those who care for the sick, the scene of the Cross provides a way of understanding that even when it seems that there is nothing more to do there remains much to do, because "remaining" by the side of the sick is a sign of love and of the hope that it contains. The proclamation of life after death is not an illusion nor merely a consolation, but a certainty lodged at the centre of love that death cannot devour.

III. THE SAMARITAN'S "HEART THAT SEES": HUMAN LIFE IS A SACRED AND INVIOLABLE GIFT

Whatever their physical or psychological condition, human persons always retain their original dignity as created in the image of God. They can live and grow in the divine splendour because they are called to exist in "the image and glory of God" (*1 Cor* 11:7; *2 Cor* 3:18). Their dignity lies in this vocation. God became man to save us, and he promises us salvation and calls us to communion with him: here lies the ultimate foundation of human dignity.[14]

It is proper for the Church to accompany with mercy the weakest in their journey of suffering, to preserve in them the theologal life, and to guide them to salvation.[15] The Church of the Good Samaritan[16] regards "the service to the sick as an integral part of its mission".[17] When understood in the perspective of communion and solidarity among human persons, the Church's salvific mediation helps to surmount reductionist and individualistic tendencies.[18]

"A heart that sees" is central to the programme of the Good Samaritan. He "teaches that it is necessary to convert the gaze of the heart, because many times the beholder does not see. Why?

---

[14] Cf. Congregation for the Doctrine of the Faith, Letter *Placuit Deo* (22nd February 2018), 6: *AAS* 110 (2018), 430.

[15] Cf. Pontifical Council for Pastoral Assistance to Health Care Workers, *New Charter for Health Care Workers*, n. 9.

[16] Cf. Paul VI, *Address during the last general meeting of the Second Vatican Council* (7th December 1965): *AAS* 58 (1966), 55-56.

[17] Pontifical Council for Pastoral Assistance to Health Care Workers, *New Charter for Health Care Workers*, n. 9.

[18] Cf. Congregation for the Doctrine of the Faith, Letter *Placuit Deo* (22nd February 2018), 12: *AAS* 110 (2018), 433-434.

Because compassion is lacking [...] Without compassion, people who look do not get involved with what they observe, and they keep going; instead people who have a compassionate heart are touched and engaged, they stop and show care".[19] This heart sees where love is needed and acts accordingly.[20] These eyes identify in weakness God's call to appreciate that human life is the primary common good of society.[21] Human life is a highest good, and society is called to acknowledge this. Life is a sacred and inviolable gift[22] and every human person, created by God, has a transcendent vocation to a unique relationship with the One who gives life. "The invisible God out of the abundance of his love"[23] offers to each and every human person a plan of salvation that allows the affirmation that: "Life is always a good. This is an instinctive perception and a fact of experience, and man is called to grasp the profound reason why this is so".[24] For this reason, the Church is always happy to collaborate with all people of good will, with believers of other confessions or religions as well as non-believers, who respect the dignity of human life, even in the last stages of suffering and death, and reject any action contrary to human life.[25] God the Creator offers life and its dignity to man

---

[19] Francis, *Address to the participants of the Plenary Session of the Congregation for the Doctrine of the Faith* (30th January 2020): *L'Osservatore Romano*, 31st January 2020, 7.

[20] Cf. Benedict XVI, Encyclical Letter *Deus caritas est* (25th December 2005), 31: *AAS* 98 (2006), 245.

[21] Cf. Benedict XVI, Encyclical Letter *Caritas in veritate* (29th June 2009), 76: *AAS* 101 (2009), 707.

[22] Cf. John Paul II, Encyclical Letter *Evangelium vitae* (25th March 1995), 49: *AAS* 87 (1995), 455. "the deepest and most authentic meaning of life: namely, that of being a gift which is fully realised in the giving of self".

[23] Second Vatican Ecumenical Council, Dogmatic Constitution *Dei verbum* (8th November 1965), 2: *AAS* 58 (1966), 818.

[24] John Paul II, Encyclical Letter *Evangelium vitae* (25th March 1995), 34: *AAS* 87 (1995), 438.

[25] Cf. *Position Paper of the Abrahamic Monotheistic Religions on matters concerning life*, Vatican City, 28th October 2019: " We oppose any form of euthanasia – that is the direct, deliberate and intentional act of taking life – as well as physician assisted suicide – that is the direct, deliberate and intentional support of committing suicide – because they fundamentally contradict the inalienable value of human life, and therefore are inherently and consequentially morally and religiously wrong, and should be forbidden without exceptions".

as a precious gift to safeguard and nurture, and ultimately to be accountable to him.

The Church affirms that the positive meaning of human life is something already knowable by right reason, and in the light of faith is confirmed and understood in its inalienable dignity.[26] This criterion is neither subjective nor arbitrary but is founded on a natural inviolable dignity. Life is the first good because it is the basis for the enjoyment of every other good including the transcendent vocation to share the trinitarian love of the living God to which every human being is called:[27] "The special love of the Creator for each human being 'confers upon him or her an infinite dignity'".[28] The uninfringeable value of life is a fundamental principle of the natural moral law and an essential foundation of the legal order. Just as we cannot make another person our slave, even if they ask to be, so we cannot directly choose to take the life of another, even if they request it. Therefore, to end the life of a sick person who requests euthanasia is by no means to acknowledge and respect their autonomy, but on the contrary to disavow the value of both their freedom, now under the sway of suffering and illness, *and* of their life by excluding any further possibility of human relationship, of sensing the meaning of their existence, or of growth in the theologal life. Moreover, it is to take the place of God in deciding the moment of death. For this reason, "abortion, euthanasia and wilful self-destruction (…) poison human society, but they do more harm to those who practise them than those who suffer from the injury. Moreover, they are a supreme dishonour to the Creator".[29]

---

[26] Cf. Francis, *Address to Participants in the Commemorative Conference of the Italian Catholic Physicians' Association on the occasion of its 70th Anniversary of foundation* (15th November 2014): *AAS* 106 (2014), 976.

[27] Cf. Pontifical Council for Pastoral Assistance to Health Care Workers, *New Charter for Health Care Workers*, n. 1; Congregation for the Doctrine of the Faith, Instruction *Dignitas personae* (8th September 2008), 8: *AAS* 100 (2008), 863.

[28] Francis, Encyclical Letter *Laudato si'* (24th May 2015), 65: *AAS* 107 (2015), 873.

[29] Second Vatican Ecumenical Council, Pastoral Constitution *Gaudium et spes* (7th December 1965), 27: *AAS* 58 (1966), 1047-1048.

IV. THE CULTURAL OBSTACLES THAT OBSCURE THE SACRED VALUE OF EVERY HUMAN LIFE

Among the obstacles that diminish our sense of the profound intrinsic value of every human life, the first lies in the notion of "dignified death" as measured by the standard of the "quality of life," which a utilitarian anthropological perspective sees in terms "primarily related to economic means, to 'well-being,' to the beauty and enjoyment of physical life, forgetting the other, more profound, interpersonal, spiritual and religious dimensions of existence".[30] In this perspective, life is viewed as worthwhile only if it has, in the judgement of the individual or of third parties, an acceptable degree of quality as measured by the possession or lack of particular psychological or physical functions, or sometimes simply by the presence of psychological discomfort. According to this view, a life whose quality seems poor does not deserve to continue. Human life is thus no longer recognised as a value in itself.

A second obstacle that obscures our recognition of the sacredness of human life is a false understanding of "compassion"[31]. In the face of seemingly "unbearable" suffering, the termination of a patient's life is justified in the name of "compassion". This so-called "compassionate" euthanasia holds that it is better to die than to suffer, and that it would be compassionate to help a patient to die by means of euthanasia or assisted suicide. In reality, human compassion consists not in

---

[30] Francis, *Address to Participants in the Commemorative Conference of the Italian Catholic Physicians' Association on the occasion of its 70th Anniversary of foundation* (15th November 2014): *AAS* 106 (2014), 976.

[31] Cf. Francis *Address to the National Federation of the Orders of Doctors and Dental Surgeons* (20th September 2019): *L'Osservatore Romano,* 21st September 2019, 8: "These are hasty ways of dealing with choices that are not, as they might seem, an expression of the person's freedom, when they include the discarding of the patient as a possibility, or false compassion in the face of the request to be helped to anticipate death".

causing death, but in embracing the sick, in supporting them in their difficulties, in offering them affection, attention, and the means to alleviate the suffering.

A third factor that hinders the recognition of the value of one's own life and the lives of others is a growing individualism within interpersonal relationships, where the other is viewed as a limitation or a threat to one's freedom. At the root of this attitude is "a neo-pelagianism in which the individual, radically autonomous, presumes to save himself, without recognising that, at the deepest level of being, he depends on God and others [...]. On the other hand, a certain neo-gnosticism puts forward a model of salvation that is merely interior, closed off in its own subjectivism",[32] that wishes to free the person from the limitations of the body, especially when it is fragile and ill.

Individualism, in particular, is at the root of what is regarded as the most hidden malady of our time: solitude or privacy.[33] It is thematised in some regulatory contexts even as a "right to solitude", beginning with the autonomy of the person and the "principle of permission-consent" which can, in certain conditions of discomfort or sickness, be extended to the choice of whether or not to continue living. This "right" underlies euthanasia and assisted suicide. The basic idea is that those who find themselves in a state of dependence and unable to realise a perfect autonomy and reciprocity, come to be cared for as a *favour* to them. The concept of the good is thus reduced to a social accord: each one receives the treatment and assistance that autonomy or social and economic utility make possible or expedient. As a result, interpersonal relationships are impoverished, becoming fragile in the absence of supernatural charity, and of that human solidarity

---

[32] Congregation for the Doctrine of the Faith, Letter *Placuit Deo* (22nd February 2018), 3: *AAS* 110 (2018), 428-429; Cf. Francis, Encyclical Letter *Laudato si'* (24th May 2015), 162: *AAS* 107 (2015), 912.

[33] Cf. Benedict XVI, Encyclical Letter *Caritas in veritate* (29th June 2009), 53: *AAS* 101 (2009), 688. "One of the deepest forms of poverty a person can experience is isolation. If we look closely at other kinds of poverty, including material forms, we see that they are born of isolation, from not being loved or from difficulties in being able to love".

and social support necessary to face the most difficult moments and decisions of life.

This way of thinking about human relationships and the significance of the good cannot but undermine the very meaning of life, facilitating its manipulation, even through laws that legalise euthanistic practices, resulting in the death of the sick. Such actions deform relationships and induce a grave insensibility toward the care of the sick person. In such circumstances, baseless moral dilemmas arise regarding what are in reality simply mandatory elements of basic care, such as feeding and hydration of terminally ill persons who are not conscious.

In this connection, Pope Francis has spoken of a "throwaway culture"[34] where the victims are the weakest human beings, who are likely to be "discarded" when the system aims for efficiency at all costs. This cultural phenomenon, which is deeply contrary to solidarity, John Paul II described as a "culture of death" that gives rise to real "structures of sin"[35] that can lead to the performance of actions wrong in themselves for the sole purpose of "feeling better" in carrying them out. A confusion between good and evil materialises in an area where every personal life should instead be understood to possess a unique and unrepeatable value with a promise of and openness to the transcendent. In this culture of waste and death, euthanasia and assisted suicide emerge as erroneous solutions to the challenge of the care of terminal patients.

---

[34] Cf. Francis, Apostolic Exhortation *Evangelii gaudium* (24th November 2013), 53: *AAS* 105 (2013), 1042; See also: Id., *Address to a delegation from the Dignitatis Humanae Institute* (7th December 2013): *AAS* 106 (2014) 14-15; Id., *Meeting of the Pope with the Elderly* (28th September 2014): *AAS* 106 (2014) 759-760.

[35] Cf. John Paul II, Encyclical Letter *Evangelium vitae* (25th March 1995), 12: *AAS* 87 (1995), 414.

V. THE TEACHING
OF THE MAGISTERIUM

1. THE PROHIBITION OF EUTHANASIA
AND ASSISTED SUICIDE

With her mission to transmit to the faithful the grace of the Redeemer and the holy law of God already discernible in the precepts of the natural moral law, the Church is obliged to intervene in order to exclude once again all ambiguity in the teaching of the Magisterium concerning euthanasia and assisted suicide, even where these practices have been legalised.

In particular, the dissemination of medical end-of-life protocols such as the *Do Not Resuscitate Order* or the *Physician Orders for Life Sustaining Treatment* – with all of their variations depending on national laws and contexts – were initially thought of as instruments to avoid aggressive medical treatment in the terminal phases of life. Today these protocols cause serious problems regarding the duty to protect the life of patients in the most critical stages of sickness. On the one hand, medical staff feel increasingly bound by the self-determination expressed in patient declarations that deprive physicians of their freedom and duty to safeguard life even where they could do so. On the other hand, in some healthcare settings, concerns have recently arisen about the widely reported abuse of such protocols viewed in a euthanistic perspective with the result that neither patients nor families are consulted in final decisions about care. This happens above all in the countries where, with the legalisation of euthanasia, wide margins of ambiguity are left open in end-of-life law regarding the meaning of obligations to provide care.

For these reasons, the Church is convinced of the necessity to reaffirm as definitive teaching that euthanasia is a *crime against human life* because, in this act, one chooses directly to cause the death of another innocent human being. The correct definition of euthanasia depends, not on a consideration of the goods or values at stake, but on the *moral object* properly specified by the choice of "an action or an omission which of itself or by intention causes death, in order that all pain may in this way be eliminated".[36] "Euthanasia's terms of reference, therefore, are to be found in the intention of the will and in the methods used".[37] The moral evaluation of euthanasia and its consequences does not depend on a balance of principles that the situation and the pain of the patient could, according to some, justify the termination of the sick person. Values of life, autonomy, and decision-making ability are not on the same level as the quality of life as such.

Euthanasia, therefore, is an intrinsically evil act, in every situation or circumstance. In the past the Church has already affirmed in a definitive way "that euthanasia is *a grave violation of the Law of God*, since it is the deliberate and morally unacceptable killing of a human person. This doctrine is based upon the natural law and upon the written Word of God, is transmitted by the Church's Tradition and taught by the ordinary and universal Magisterium. Depending on the circumstances, this practice involves the malice proper to suicide or murder".[38] *Any formal or immediate material cooperation* in such an act is a grave sin against human life: "No authority can legitimately recommend or permit such an action. For it is a question of the violation of the divine law, an offence against the dignity of the human person, a crime against

---

[36] Congregation for the Doctrine of the Faith, Declaration *Iura et bona* (5th May 1980), II: *AAS* 72 (1980), 546.

[37] John Paul II, Encyclical Letter *Evangelium vitae* (25th March 1995), 65: *AAS* 87 (1995), 475; cf. Congregation for the Doctrine of the Faith, Declaration *Iura et bona* (5th May 1980), II: *AAS* 72 (1980), 546.

[38] John Paul II, Encyclical Letter *Evangelium vitae* (25th March 1995), 65: *AAS* 87 (1995), 477. It is a definitively proposed doctrine in which the Church commits her infallibility: cf. Congregation for the Doctrine of the Faith, *Doctrinal Commentary on the Concluding Formula of the Professio Fidei* (29th June 1998), 11: *AAS* 90 (1998), 550.

life, and an attack on humanity".[39] Therefore, euthanasia is an act of homicide that no end can justify and that does not tolerate any form of complicity or active or passive collaboration. Those who approve laws of euthanasia and assisted suicide, therefore, become accomplices of a grave sin that others will execute. They are also guilty of scandal because by such laws they contribute to the distortion of conscience, even among the faithful.[40]

Each life has the same value and dignity for everyone: the respect for the life of another is the same as the respect owed to one's own life. One who chooses with full liberty to take his or her own life breaks his or her relationship with God and with others, and renounces him- or herself as a moral subject. Assisted suicide aggravates the gravity of this act because it implicates another in one's own despair. Another person is led to turn his will from the mystery of God in the theological virtue of hope and thus to repudiate the authentic value of life and to break the covenant that establishes the human family. Assisting in a suicide is an unjustified collaboration in an unlawful act that contradicts the theologal relationship with God and the moral relationship that unites us with others who share the gift of life and the meaning of existence.

When a request for euthanasia rises from anguish and despair,[41] "although in these cases the guilt of the individual may be reduced, or completely absent, nevertheless the error of judgement into which the conscience falls, perhaps in good faith, does not change the nature of this act of killing, which will always be in itself something to be rejected".[42] The same applies

---

[39] Congregation for the Doctrine of the Faith, Declaration *Iura et bona* (5th May 1980), II: *AAS* 72 (1980), 546.

[40] Cf. *Catechism of the Catholic Church*, 2286.

[41] Cf. *Catechism of the Catholic Church*, 1735 and 2282.

[42] Congregation for the Doctrine of the Faith, Declaration *Iura et bona* (5th May 1980), II: *AAS* 72 (1980), 546.

to assisted suicide. Such actions are never a real service to the patient, but a help to die.

Euthanasia and assisted suicide are always the wrong choice: "the medical personnel and the other health care workers – faithful to the task 'always to be at the service of life and to assist it up until the very end' – cannot give themselves to any euthanistic practice, neither at the request of the interested party, and much less that of the family. In fact, since there is no right to dispose of one's life arbitrarily, no health care worker can be compelled to execute a non-existent right".[43]

This is why *euthanasia and assisted suicide are a defeat* for those who theorise about them, who decide upon them, or who practise them.[44]

For this reason, it is gravely unjust to enact laws that legalise euthanasia or justify and support suicide, invoking the false right to choose a death improperly characterised as respectable only because it is chosen.[45] Such laws strike at the foundation of the legal order: the right to life sustains all other rights, including the exercise of freedom. The existence of such laws deeply wounds human relations and justice, and threatens the mutual trust among human beings. The legitimisation of assisted suicide and euthanasia is a sign of the degradation of legal systems. Pope Francis recalls that "the current socio-cultural context is gradually eroding the awareness of what makes human life precious. In fact, it is increasingly valued on the basis of its efficiency and utility, to the point of considering as 'discarded lives' or 'unworthy lives' those who do not meet this criterion. In this situation of the loss of authentic values, the mandatory obligations of solidarity and of human and Christian

---

[43] Pontifical Council for Pastoral Assistance to Health Care Workers, *New Charter for Health Care Workers*, n. 169.

[44] Cf. *Ibid.*, 170.

[45] Cf. John Paul II, Encyclical Letter *Evangelium vitae* (25th March 1995), 72: *AAS* 87 (1995), 484-485.

fraternity also fail. In reality, a society deserves the status of 'civil' if it develops antibodies against the culture of waste; if it recognises the intangible value of human life; if solidarity is factually practised and safeguarded as a foundation for living together".[46] In some countries of the world, tens of thousands of people have already died by euthanasia, and many of them because they displayed psychological suffering or depression. Physicians themselves report that abuses frequently occur when the lives of persons who would never have desired euthanasia are terminated. The request for death is in many cases itself a symptom of disease, aggravated by isolation and discomfort. The Church discerns in these difficulties an occasion for a spiritual purification that allows hope to become truly theological when it is focused on God and only on God.

Rather than indulging in a spurious condescension, the Christian must offer to the sick the help they need to shake off their despair. The commandment "do not kill" (*Ex* 20:13; *Dt* 5:17) is in fact a *yes to life* which God guarantees, and it "becomes a call to attentive love which protects and promotes the life of one's neighbour".[47] The Christian therefore knows that earthly life is not the supreme value. Ultimate happiness is in heaven. Thus the Christian will not expect physical life to continue when death is evidently near. The Christian must help the dying to break free from despair and to place their hope in God.

From a clinical perspective, the factors that largely determine requests for euthanasia and assisted suicide are unmanaged pain, and the loss of human and theological hope, provoked by the often inadequate psychological and spiritual human assistance provided by those who care for the sick.[48]

---

[46] Francis, *Address to the Participants of the Plenary Session of the Congregation for the Doctrine of the Faith* (30th January 2020): *L'Osservatore Romano*, 31st January 2020, 7.

[47] John Paul II, Encyclical Letter *Veritatis splendor* (6th August 1993), 15: *AAS* 85 (1993), 1145.

[48] Cf. Benedict XVI, Encyclical Letter *Spe salvi* (30th November 2007), 36, 37: *AAS* 99 (2007), 1014-1016.

Experience confirms that "the pleas of gravely ill people who sometimes ask for death are not to be understood as implying a true desire for euthanasia; in fact, it is almost always a case of an anguished plea for help and love. What a sick person needs, besides medical care, is love, the human and supernatural warmth with which sick persons can and ought to be surrounded by all those close to him or her, parents and children, doctors and nurses".[49] A sick person, surrounded by a loving human and Christian presence, can overcome all forms of depression and need not succumb to the anguish of loneliness and abandonment to suffering and death.

One experiences pain not just as a biological fact to be managed in order to make it bearable, but as the mystery of human vulnerability in the face of the end of physical life — a difficult event to endure, given that the unity of the body and the soul is essential to the human person.

Therefore, the "end of life", inevitably presaged by pain and suffering, can be faced with dignity only by the re-signification of the event of death itself — by opening it to the horizon of eternal life and affirming the transcendent destiny of each person. In fact, "suffering is something which is *still wider* than sickness, more complex, and at the same time still more deeply rooted in humanity itself".[50] With the help of grace this suffering can, like the suffering of Christ on the Cross, be animated from within with divine charity.

Those who assist persons with chronic illnesses or in the terminal stages of life must be able to "know how to stay", to keep vigil, with those who suffer the anguish of death, "to console" them, to be with them in their loneliness, to be an *abiding with* that

---

[49] Congregation for the Doctrine of the Faith, Declaration *Iura et bona* (5th May 1980), II: *AAS* 72 (1980), 546.

[50] John Paul II, Apostolic Letter *Salvifici doloris* (11th February 1984), 5: *AAS* 76 (1984), 204.

can instil hope.[51] By means of the faith and charity expressed in the intimacy of the soul, the caregiver can experience the pain of another, can be open to a personal relationship with the weak that expands the horizons of life beyond death, and thus can become a presence full of hope.

"Weep with those who weep" (*Rm* 12:15): for blessed is the one whose compassion includes shedding tears with others (cf. *Mt* 5:4). Love is made possible and suffering given meaning in relationships where persons share in solidarity the human condition and the journey to God, and are joined in a covenant[52] that enables them to glimpse the light beyond death. Medical care occurs within the *therapeutic covenant* between the physician and the patient who are united in the recognition of the transcendent value of life and the mystical meaning of suffering. In the light of this covenant, good medical care can be valued, while the utilitarian and individualistic vision that prevails today can be dispelled.

2. THE MORAL OBLIGATION TO EXCLUDE AGGRESSIVE MEDICAL TREATMENT

The Magisterium of the Church recalls that, when one approaches the end of earthly existence, the dignity of the human person entails the right to die with the greatest possible serenity and with one's proper human and Christian dignity intact.[53] To precipitate death or delay it through "aggressive medical treatments"

---

[51] Cf. Benedict XVI, Encyclical Letter *Spe salvi* (30th November 2007), 38: *AAS* 99 (2007), 1016.

[52] Cf. John Paul II, Apostolic Letter *Salvifici doloris* (11th February 1984), 29: *AAS* 76 (1984), 244: "the person who is 'a neighbour' cannot indifferently pass by the suffering of another: this in the name of fundamental human solidarity, still more in the name of love of neighbour. He must 'stop,' 'sympathise,' just like the Samaritan of the Gospel parable. The parable in itself expresses *a deeply Christian truth*, but one that at the same time is very universally human."

[53] Cf. Congregation for the Doctrine of the Faith, Declaration *Iura et bona* (5th May 1980), IV: *AAS* 72 (1980), 549-551.

deprives death of its due dignity.[54] Medicine today can artificially delay death, often without real benefit to the patient. When death is imminent, and without interruption of the normal care the patient requires in such cases, it is lawful according to science and conscience to renounce treatments that provide only a precarious or painful extension of life.[55] It is not lawful to suspend treatments that are required to maintain essential physiological functions, as long as the body can benefit from them (such as hydration, nutrition, thermoregulation, proportionate respiratory support, and the other types of assistance needed to maintain bodily homeostasis and manage systemic and organic pain). The suspension of futile treatments *must not involve the withdrawal of therapeutic care*. This clarification is now indispensable in light of the numerous court cases in recent years that have led to the withdrawal of care from – and to the early death of – critically but not terminally ill patients, for whom it was decided to suspend life-sustaining care which would not improve the quality of life.

In the specific case of aggressive medical treatment, it should be repeated that the renunciation of extraordinary and/ or disproportionate means "is not the equivalent of suicide or euthanasia; it rather expresses acceptance of the human condition in the face of death"[56] or a deliberate decision to waive

---

[54] Cf. *Catechism of the Catholic Church*, 2278; Pontifical Council for Pastoral Assistance to Health Care Workers, *The Charter for Health Care Workers*, Vatican City, 1995, n. 119; John Paul II, Encyclical Letter *Evangelium vitae* (25th March 1995), 65: *AAS* 87 (1995), 475; Francis, *Message to the participants in the European regional meeting of the World Medical Association* (7th November 2017). "And even if we know that we cannot always guarantee healing or a cure, we can and must always care for the living, without ourselves shortening their life, but also without futilely resisting their death"; Pontifical Council for Pastoral Assistance to Health Care Workers, *New Charter for Health Care Workers*, n. 149.

[55] Cf. *Catechism of the Catholic Church*, 2278; Congregation for the Doctrine of the Faith, Declaration *Iura et bona* (5th May 1980), IV: *AAS* 72 (1980), 550-551; John Paul II, Encyclical Letter *Evangelium vitae* (25th March 1995), 65: *AAS* 87 (1995), 475; Pontifical Council for Pastoral Assistance to Health Care Workers, *New Charter for Health Care Workers*, n. 150.

[56] John Paul II, Encyclical Letter *Evangelium vitae* (25th March 1995), 65: *AAS* 87 (1995), 476.

disproportionate medical treatments which have little hope of positive results. The renunciation of treatments that would only provide a precarious and painful prolongation of life can also mean respect for the will of the dying person as expressed in advanced directives for treatment, *excluding however every act of a euthanistic or suicidal nature.*[57]

The principle of proportionality refers to the overall well-being of the sick person. To choose among values (for example, life versus quality of life) involves an erroneous moral judgement when it excludes from consideration the safeguarding of personal integrity, the good life, and the true moral object of the act undertaken.[58] Every medical action must always have as its object—intended by the moral agent—the promotion of life and never the pursuit of death.[59] The physician is never a mere executor of the will of patients or their legal representatives, but retains the right and obligation to withdraw at will from any course of action contrary to the moral good discerned by conscience.[60]

3. BASIC CARE: THE REQUIREMENT OF NUTRITION AND HYDRATION

A fundamental and inescapable principle of the assistance of the critically or terminally ill person is the *continuity of care* for the essential physiological functions. In particular, required basic care for each person includes the administration of the nourishment and fluids needed to maintain bodily homeostasis,

---

[57] Cf. Pontifical Council for Pastoral Assistance to Health Care Workers, *New Charter for Health Care Workers*, n. 150.

[58] Cf. John Paul II, *Speech to participants in a study seminar on responsible procreation* (5th June 1987), n. 1: *Insegnamenti di Giovanni Paolo II* X/2 (1987), 1962: "To speak of a 'conflict of values or goods' and of the consequent need to perform some sort of 'balance' of them, choosing one and refuting the other, is not morally correct".

[59] Cf. John Paul II, *Address to the Italian Catholic Doctors Association* (28th December 1978): *Insegnamenti di Giovanni Paolo II*, I (1978), 438.

[60] Cf. Pontifical Council for Pastoral Assistance to Health Care Workers, *New Charter for Health Care Workers*, n. 150.

insofar as and until this demonstrably attains the purpose of providing hydration and nutrition for the patient.[61]

When the provision of nutrition and hydration no longer benefits the patient, because the patient's organism either cannot absorb them or cannot metabolise them, their administration should be suspended. In this way, one does not unlawfully hasten death through the deprivation of the hydration and nutrition vital for bodily function, but nonetheless respects the natural course of the critical or terminal illness. The withdrawal of this sustenance is an unjust action that can cause great suffering to the one who has to endure it. Nutrition and hydration do not constitute medical therapy in a proper sense, which is intended to counteract the pathology that afflicts the patient. They are instead forms of obligatory care of the patient, representing both a primary clinical and an unavoidable human response to the sick person. Obligatory nutrition and hydration can at times be administered artificially,[62] provided that it does not cause harm or intolerable suffering to the patient.[63]

4. PALLIATIVE CARE

Continuity of care is part of the enduring responsibility to appreciate the needs of the sick person: care needs, pain relief, and affective and spiritual needs. As demonstrated by vast clinical experience, palliative medicine constitutes a precious and crucial instrument in the care of patients during

---

[61] Cf. Congregation for the Doctrine of the Faith, *Responses to certain questions of the United States Conference of Catholic Bishops concerning artificial nutrition and hydration* (1st August 2007): *AAS* 99 (2007), 820.

[62] Cf. *Ibid.*

[63] Cf. Pontifical Council for Pastoral Assistance to Health Care Workers, *New Charter for Health Care Workers*, n. 152: "Nutrition and hydration, even if administered artificially, are classified as basic care owed to the dying person when they do not prove to be too burdensome or without any benefit. The unjustified discontinuation thereof can be tantamount to a real act of euthanasia: 'The administration of food and water even by artificial means is, in principle, an ordinary and proportionate means of preserving life. It is therefore obligatory to the extent which, and for as long as, it is shown to accomplish its proper finality, which is hydration and nourishment of the patient. In this way, suffering and death by starvation and dehydration are prevented'".

the most painful, agonising, chronic and terminal stages of illness. *Palliative care* is an authentic expression of the human and Christian activity of providing care, the tangible symbol of the compassionate "remaining" at the side of the suffering person. Its goal is "to alleviate suffering in the final stages of illness and at the same time to ensure the patient appropriate human accompaniment"[64] improving quality of life and overall well-being as much as possible and in a dignified manner. Experience teaches us that the employment of palliative care reduces considerably the number of persons who request euthanasia. To this end, a resolute commitment is desirable to extend palliative treatments to those who need them, within the limits of what is fiscally possible, and to assist them in the terminal stages of life, but as an *integrated approach to the care* of existing chronic or degenerative pathologies involving a complex prognosis that is unfavourable and painful for the patient and family.[65]

Palliative care should include spiritual assistance for patients and their families. Such assistance inspires faith and hope in God in the terminally ill as well as their families whom it helps to accept the death of their loved one. It is an essential contribution that is offered by pastoral workers and the whole Christian community. According to the model of the Good Samaritan, acceptance overcomes denial, and hope prevails over anguish,[66] particularly when, as the end draws near, suffering is protracted by a worsening pathology. In this phase, the identification of an effective pain relief therapy allows the patient to face the sickness and death without the fear of undergoing intolerable pain. Such care must be accompanied by a fraternal

---

[64] Francis, *Address to participants in the plenary of the Pontifical Academy for Life* (5th March 2015): *AAS* 107 (2015), 274, with reference to: John Paul II, Encyclical Letter *Evangelium vitae* (25th March 1995), 65: *AAS* 87 (1995), 476. Cf. *Catechism of the Catholic Church*, 2279.

[65] Cf. Francis, *Address to participants in the plenary of the Pontifical Academy for Life* (5th March 2015): *AAS* 107 (2015), 275.

[66] Cf. Pontifical Council for Pastoral Assistance to Health Care Workers, *New Charter for Health Care Workers*, n. 147.

support to reduce the loneliness that patients feel when they are insufficiently supported or understood in their difficulties.

Palliative care cannot provide a fundamental answer to suffering or eradicate it from people's lives.[67] To claim otherwise is to generate a false hope, and cause even greater despair in the midst of suffering. Medical science can understand physical pain better and can deploy the best technical resources to treat it. But terminal illness causes a profound suffering in the sick person, who seeks a level of care beyond the purely technical. *Spe salvi facti sumus*: in hope, theological hope, directed toward God, we have been saved, says Saint Paul (*Rm* 8:24).

"The wine of hope" is the specific contribution of the Christian faith in the care of the sick and refers to the way in which God overcomes evil in the world. In times of suffering, the human person should be able to experience a solidarity and a love that takes on the suffering, offering a sense of life that extends beyond death. All of this has a great social importance: "A society unable to accept the suffering of its members and incapable of helping to share their suffering, and to bear it inwardly through 'compassion' is a cruel and inhuman society".[68]

It should be recognised, however, that the definition of palliative care has in recent years taken on a sometimes equivocal connotation. In some countries, national laws regulating palliative care (*Palliative Care Act*) as well as the laws on the "end of life" (*End-of-Life Law*) provide, along with palliative treatments, something called Medical Assistance in Dying (MAiD) that can include the possibility of requesting euthanasia and assisted suicide. Such legal provisions are a cause of grave cultural confusion: by including under palliative care the

---

[67] Cf. John Paul II, Apostolic Letter *Salvifici doloris* (11th February 1984), 2: *AAS* 76 (1984), 202: "Suffering seems to belong to man's transcendence: it is one of those points in which man in a certain sense 'destined' to go beyond himself, and he is called to this in a mysterious way".

[68] Benedict XVI, Encyclical Letter *Spe salvi* (30th November 2007), 38: *AAS* 99 (2007), 1016.

provision of integrated medical assistance for a voluntary death, they imply that it would be morally lawful to request euthanasia or assisted suicide.

In addition, palliative interventions to reduce the suffering of gravely or terminally ill patients in these regulatory contexts can involve the administration of medications that intend to hasten death, as well as the suspension or interruption of hydration and nutrition even when death is not imminent. In fact, such practices are equivalent to a *direct action or omission to bring about death and are therefore unlawful*. The growing diffusion of such legislation and of scientific guidelines of national and international professional societies, constitutes a socially irresponsible threat to many people, including a growing number of vulnerable persons who needed only to be better cared for and comforted but are instead being led to choose euthanasia and suicide.

5. THE ROLE OF THE FAMILY AND HOSPICE

The role of the family is central to the care of the terminally ill patient.[69] In the family a person can count on strong relationships, valued in themselves apart from their helpfulness or the joy they bring. It is essential that the sick under care do not feel themselves to be a burden, but can sense the intimacy and support of their loved ones. The family needs help and adequate resources to fulfil this mission. Recognising the family's primary, fundamental and irreplaceable social function, governments should undertake to provide the necessary resources and structures to support it. In addition, Christian-inspired healthcare facilities should not neglect but instead integrate the family's human and spiritual accompaniment in *a unified programme of care for the sick person*.

Next to the family, *hospice centres* which welcome the terminally sick and ensure their care until the last moment of

---

[69] Cf. Francis, Apostolic Exhortation *Amoris laetitia* (19th March 2016), 48: *AAS* 108 (2016), 330.

life provide an important and valuable service. After all, "the Christian response to the mystery of death and suffering is to provide not an explanation but a Presence"[70] that shoulders the pain, accompanies it, and opens it to a trusting hope. These centres are an example of genuine humanity in society, sanctuaries where suffering is full of meaning. For this reason, they must be staffed by qualified personnel, possess the proper resources, and always be open to families. "In this regard, I think about how well *hospice* does for palliative care, where terminally ill people are accompanied with qualified medical, psychological and spiritual support, so that they can live with dignity, comforted by the closeness of loved ones, in the final phase of their earthly life. I hope that these centres continue to be places where the 'therapy of dignity' is practised with commitment, thus nurturing love and respect for life."[71] In these settings, as well as in Catholic facilities, healthcare workers and pastoral staff, in addition to being clinically competent, should also be practising an authentic theologal life of faith and hope that is directed towards God, for this constitutes the highest form of the humanisation of dying.[72]

6. ACCOMPANIMENT AND CARE IN PRE-NATAL AND PAEDIATRIC MEDICINE

Regarding the care of neo-natal infants and children suffering from terminal chronic-degenerative diseases, or are in the terminal stages of life itself, it is necessary to reaffirm what follows, aware of the need for first-rate programmes that ensure the well-being of the children and their families.

---

[70] C. Saunders, *Watch with Me: Inspiration for a life in hospice care*, Observatory House, Lancaster, UK, 2005, 29.

[71] Francis, *Address to the Participants of the Plenary Session of the Congregation for the Doctrine of the Faith* (30th January 2020): *L'Osservatore Romano*, 31st January 2020, 7.

[72] Cf. Pontifical Council for Pastoral Assistance to Health Care Workers, *New Charter for Health Care Workers*, n. 148.

Beginning at conception, children suffering from malformation or other pathologies are *little patients* whom medicine today can always assist and accompany in a manner respectful of life. Their life is sacred, unique, unrepeatable, and inviolable, exactly like that of every adult person.

Children suffering from so-called pre-natal pathologies "incompatible with life" – that will surely end in death within a short period of time – and in the absence of foetal or neo-natal therapies capable of improving their health, should not be left without assistance, but must be accompanied like any other patient until they reach natural death. *Pre-natal comfort care* favours a path of *integrated assistance* involving the support of medical staff and pastoral care workers alongside the constant presence of the family. The child is a special patient and requires the care of a professional with expert medical knowledge and affective skills. The empathetic accompaniment of a child, who is among the most frail, in the terminal stages of life, aims to give life to the years of a child and not years to the child's life.

Pre-natal Hospice Centres, in particular, provide an essential support to families who welcome the birth of a child in a fragile condition. In these centres, competent medical assistance, spiritual accompaniment, and the support of other families, who have undergone the same experience of pain and loss, constitute an essential resource. It is the pastoral duty of Christian-inspired healthcare workers to make efforts to expand the accessibility of these centres throughout the world.

These forms of assistance are particularly necessary for those children who, given the current state of scientific knowledge, are destined to die soon after birth or within a short period of time. Providing care for these children helps the parents to handle their grief and to regard this experience not just as a loss, but as a moment in the journey of love which they have travelled together with their child.

39

Unfortunately the dominant culture today does not encourage this approach. The sometimes obsessive recourse to pre-natal diagnosis, along with the emergence of a culture unfriendly to disability, often prompts the choice of abortion, going so far as to portray it as a kind of "prevention." Abortion consists in the deliberate killing of an innocent human life and as such it is never lawful. The use of pre-natal diagnosis for selective purposes is contrary to the dignity of the person and gravely unlawful because it expresses a eugenic mentality. In other cases, after birth, the same culture encourages the suspension or non-initiation of care for the child as soon as it is born because a disability is present or may develop in the future. This utilitarian approach—inhumane and gravely immoral—cannot be countenanced.

The fundamental principle of paediatric care is that children in the final stages of life have the right to the respect and care due to persons. To be avoided are both aggressive medical treatment and unreasonable tenacity, as well as intentional hastening of their death. From a Christian perspective, the pastoral care of a terminally ill child demands participation in the divine life in Baptism and in Confirmation.

It may happen that pharmacological or other therapies, designed to combat the pathology from which a child suffers, are suspended during the terminal stage of an incurable disease. The attending physician may determine that the child's deteriorated clinical condition renders these therapies either futile or extreme, and possibly the cause of added suffering. Nonetheless, in such situations the integral care of the child, in its various physiological, psychological, affective and spiritual dimensions, must never cease. Care means more than therapy and healing. When a therapy is suspended because it no longer benefits an incurable patient, treatments that support the essential physiological functions of the child must continue insofar as the organism can benefit from them (hydration, nutrition, thermoregulation, proportionate respiratory support, and other types of assistance needed to maintain bodily homeostasis and manage systemic and organic pain). The desire to abstain from any overly tenacious administration of treatments deemed ineffective *should not entail the withdrawal of care.* The path of accompaniment until the moment of death must remain open. Routine interventions like respiratory assistance can be provided painlessly and proportionately. Thus appropriate care must be customised to the personal needs of the patient, to avoid that a just concern for life does not contrast with an unjust imposition of pain that could be avoided.

Evaluation and management of the physical pain of a newborn or a child show the proper respect and assistance they deserve during the difficult stages of their illness. The tender personalised care that is attested today in clinical paediatric medicine, sustained by the presence of the parents, makes possible an integrated management of care that is more effective than invasive treatments.

Maintaining the emotional bond between the parent and the child is an integral part of the process of care. The connection between caregiving and parent-child assistance that is fundamental to the treatment of incurable or terminal pathologies should be favoured as much as possible. In addition to emotional support, the spiritual moment must not be overlooked. The prayer of the people close to the sick child has a supernatural value that surpasses and deepens the affective relationship.

The ethical/juridical concept of "the best interest of the child" – when used in the cost-benefit calculations of care – can in no way form the foundation for decisions to shorten life in order to prevent suffering if these decisions envision actions or omissions that are euthanistic by nature or intention. As already mentioned, the suspension of disproportionate therapies cannot justify the suspension of the basic care, including pain relief, necessary to accompany these little patients to a dignified natural death, nor to the interruption of that spiritual care offered for one who will soon meet God.

7. ANALGESIC THERAPY
AND LOSS OF CONSCIOUSNESS

Some specialised care requires, on the part of the healthcare workers, a particular attention and competence to attain the best medical practice from an ethical point of view, with attention to people in their concrete situations of pain.

To mitigate a patient's pain, analgesic therapy employs pharmaceutical drugs that can induce loss of consciousness (sedation). While a deep religious sense can make it possible for a patient to live with pain through the lens of redemption as a special offering to God,[73] the Church nonetheless affirms the moral liceity of sedation as part of patient care in order to ensure that the end of life arrives with the greatest possible peace and in the best internal conditions. This holds also for treatments that hasten the moment of death (deep palliative sedation in the terminal stage),[74] always, to the extent possible, with the patient's informed consent. From a pastoral point of view, prior spiritual preparation of the patients should be provided in order

---

[73] Cf. Pius XII, *Responses to three religious and moral questions concerning analgesia* (24th February 1957): *AAS* 49 (1957) 134-136; Congregation for the Doctrine of the Faith, Declaration *Iura et bona* (5th May 1980), III: *AAS* 72 (1980), 547; John Paul II, Apostolic Letter *Salvifici doloris* (11th February 1984), 19: *AAS* 76 (1984), 226.

[74] Cf. Pius XII, *Speech to the first General Assembly of the Collegium Internationale Neuro-Psycho-Pharmacologicum* (9th September 1958): *AAS* 50 (1958), 694; Congregation for the Doctrine of the Faith, Declaration *Iura et bona* (5th May 1980), III: *AAS* 72 (1980), 548; *Catechism of the Catholic Church*, 2779; Pontifical Council for Pastoral Assistance to Health Care Workers, *New Charter for Health Care Workers*, n. 155 "Moreover there is the possibility of painkillers and narcotics causing a loss of consciousness in the dying person. Such usage deserves particular consideration. In the presence of unbearable pain that is resistant to typical pain-management therapies, if the moment of death is near or if there are good reasons for anticipating a particular crisis at the moment of death, a serious clinical indication may involve, with the sick person's consent, the administration of drugs that cause the loss of consciousness. This deep palliative sedation in the terminal phase, when clinically motivated, can be morally acceptable provided that it is done with the patient's consent, appropriate information is given to the family members, that any intention of euthanasia is ruled out, and that the patient has been able to perform his moral, familial and religious duties: 'As they approach death people ought to be able to satisfy their moral and family duties, and above all they ought to be able to prepare in a fully conscious way for their definitive meeting with God'. Therefore, 'it is not right to deprive the dying person of consciousness without a serious reason'".

that they may consciously approach death as an encounter with God.[75] The use of analgesics is, therefore, part of the care of the patient, but any administration that directly and intentionally causes death is a euthanistic practice and is unacceptable.[76] The sedation must exclude, as its direct purpose, the intention to kill, even though it may accelerate the inevitable onset of death.[77]

In paediatric settings, when a child (for example, a new-born) is unable to understand, it must be stated that it would be a mistake to suppose that the child can tolerate the pain, when in fact there are ways to alleviate it. Caregivers are obliged to alleviate the child's suffering as much as possible, so that he or she can reach a natural death peacefully, while being able to experience the loving presence of the medical staff and above all the family.

8. THE VEGETATIVE STATE AND THE STATE OF MINIMAL CONSCIOUSNESS

Other relevant situations are that of the patient with the persistent lack of consciousness, the so-called "vegetative state" or that of the patient in the state of "minimal consciousness". It is always completely false to assume that the vegetative state, and the state of minimal consciousness, in subjects who can breathe autonomously, are signs that the patient has ceased to be a human person with all of the dignity belonging to persons as

---

[75] Cf. Pius XII, *Responses to three religious and moral questions concerning analgesia* (24th February 1957): *AAS* 49 (1957) 145; Congregation for the Doctrine of the Faith, Declaration *Iura et bona* (5th May 1980), III: *AAS* 72 (1980), 548; John Paul II, Encyclical Letter *Evangelium vitae* (25th March 1995), 65: *AAS* 87 (1995), 476.

[76] Cf. Francis, *Address to Participants in the Commemorative Conference of the Italian Catholic Physicians' Association on the occasion of its 70th Anniversary of foundation* (15th November 2014): *AAS* 106 (2014), 978.

[77] Cf. Pius XII, *Responses to three religious and moral questions concerning analgesia* (24th February 1957): *AAS* 49 (1957), 146; Id., *Speech to the first General Assembly of the Collegium Internationale Neuro-Psycho-Pharmacologicum* (9th September 1958): *AAS* 50 (1958), 695; Congregation for the Doctrine of the Faith, Declaration *Iura et bona*, III: *AAS* 72 (1980), 548; *Catechism of the Catholic Church*, 2279; John Paul II, Encyclical Letter *Evangelium vitae* (25th March 1995), 65: *AAS* 87 (1995), 476; Pontifical Council for Pastoral Assistance to Health Care Workers, *New Charter for Health Care Workers*, n. 154.

such[78]. On the contrary, in these states of greatest weakness, the person must be acknowledged in their intrinsic value and assisted with suitable care. The fact that the sick person can remain for years in this anguishing situation without any prospect of recovery undoubtedly entails suffering for the caregivers.

One must never forget in such painful situations that the patient in these states has the right to nutrition and hydration, even administered by artificial methods that accord with the principle of ordinary means. In some cases, such measures can become disproportionate, because their administration is ineffective, or involves procedures that create an excessive burden with negative results that exceed any benefits to the patient.

In the light of these principles, the obligation of caregivers includes not just the patient, but extends to the family or to the person responsible for the patient's care, and should be comprised of adequate pastoral accompaniment. Adequate support must be provided to the families who bear the burden of long-term care for persons in these states. The support should seek to allay their discouragement and help them to avoid seeing the cessation of treatment as their only option. Caregivers must be sufficiently prepared for such situations, as family members need to be properly supported.

9. CONSCIENTIOUS OBJECTIONS ON THE PART OF HEALTHCARE WORKERS AND OF CATHOLIC HEALTHCARE INSTITUTIONS

In the face of the legalisation of euthanasia or assisted suicide – even when viewed simply as another form of medical assistance – formal or immediate material cooperation must be excluded. Such situations offer specific occasions for Christian witness

---

[78] Cf. John Paul II, *Address to the participants in the International Congress "Life sustaining treatments and vegetative state. Scientific progress and ethical dilemmas"* (20th March 2004), 3: *AAS* 96 (2004), 487: "A man, even if seriously ill or disabled in the exercise of his highest functions, is and always will be a man, and he will never become a 'vegetable' or an 'animal'".

where "we must obey God rather than men" (*Acts* 5:29). There is no right to suicide nor to euthanasia: laws exist, not to cause death, but to protect life and to facilitate coexistence among human beings. It is therefore never morally lawful to collaborate with such immoral actions or to imply collusion in word, action or omission. The one authentic right is that the sick person be accompanied and cared for with genuine humanity. Only in this way can the patient's dignity be preserved until the moment of natural death. "No health care worker, therefore, can become the defender of a non-existing right, even if euthanasia were requested by the subject in question when he was fully conscious".[79]

In this regard, the general principles regarding cooperation with evil, that is, with unlawful actions, are thus reaffirmed: "Christians, like all people of good will, are called, with a grave obligation of conscience, not to lend their formal collaboration to those practices which, although allowed by civil legislation, are in contrast with the Law of God. In fact, from the moral point of view, it is never licit formally to cooperate in evil. This cooperation occurs when the action taken, either by its very nature or by the configuration it is assuming in a concrete context, qualifies as direct participation in an act against innocent human life, or as sharing the immoral intention of the principal agent. This cooperation can never be justified either by invoking respect for the freedom of others, nor by relying on the fact that civil law provides for it and requires it: for the acts that each person personally performs, there is, in fact, a moral responsibility that no one can ever escape and on which each one will be judged by God himself (cf. *Rm* 2:6; 14:12)".[80]

Governments must acknowledge the right to conscientious objection in the medical and healthcare field, where the principles of the natural moral law are involved and especially where in the

---

[79] Pontifical Council for Pastoral Assistance to Health Care Workers, *New Charter for Health Care Workers*, n. 151.

[80] *Ibid.*, n. 151; John Paul II, Encyclical Letter *Evangelium vitae* (25th March 1995), 74: *AAS* 87 (1995), 487.

service to life the voice of conscience is daily invoked.[81] Where this is not recognised, one may be confronted with the obligation to disobey human law, in order to avoid adding one wrong to another, thereby conditioning one's conscience. Healthcare workers should not hesitate to ask for this right as a specific contribution to the common good.

Likewise, healthcare institutions must resist the strong economic pressures that may sometimes induce them to accept the practice of euthanasia. If the difficulty in finding necessary operating funds creates an enormous burden for these public institutions, then the whole society must accept an additional liability in order to ensure that the incurably ill are not left to their own or their families' resources. All of this requires that episcopal conferences and local churches, as well as Catholic communities and institutions, adopt a clear and unified position to safeguard the right of conscientious objection in regulatory contexts where euthanasia and suicide are sanctioned.

Catholic healthcare institutions constitute a concrete sign of the way in which the ecclesial community takes care of the sick following the example of the Good Samaritan. The command of Jesus to "cure the sick," (*Lk* 10:9) is fulfilled not only by laying hands on them, but also by rescuing them from the streets, assisting them in their own homes, and creating special structures of hospitality and welcome. Faithful to the command of the Lord, the Church through the centuries has created various structures where medical care finds its specific form in the context of integral service to the sick person.

Catholic healthcare institutions are called to witness faithfully to the inalienable commitment to ethics and to the fundamental human and Christian values that constitute their identity. This witness requires that they abstain from plainly immoral conduct

---

[81] Cf. Francis, *Address to Participants in the Commemorative Conference of the Italian Catholic Physicians' Association on the occasion of its 70th Anniversary of foundation* (15th November 2014): *AAS* 106 (2014), 977.

and that they affirm their formal adherence to the teachings of the ecclesial Magisterium. Any action that does not correspond to the purpose and values which inspire Catholic healthcare institutions is not morally acceptable and endangers the identification of the institution itself as "Catholic."

Institutional collaboration with other hospital systems is not morally permissible when it involves referrals for persons who request euthanasia. Such choices cannot be morally accepted or supported in their concrete realisation, even if they are legally admissible. Indeed, it can rightly be said of laws that permit euthanasia that "not only do they create no obligation for the conscience, but instead there is a grave and clear obligation to oppose them by conscientious objection. From the very beginnings of the Church, the apostolic preaching reminded Christians of their duty to obey legitimately constituted public authorities (cf. *Rm* 13:1-7; *1 Pt* 2:13-14), but at the same time firmly warned that 'we must obey God rather than men' (*Acts* 5:29)".[82]

The right to conscientious objection does not mean that Christians reject these laws in virtue of private religious conviction, but by reason of an inalienable right essential to the common good of the whole society. They are in fact laws contrary to natural law because they undermine the very foundations of human dignity and human coexistence rooted in justice.

10. PASTORAL ACCOMPANIMENT AND THE SUPPORT OF THE SACRAMENTS

Death is a decisive moment in the human person's encounter with God the Saviour. The Church is called to accompany spiritually the faithful in the situation, offering them the "healing resources" of prayer and the sacraments. Helping the Christian to experience this moment with spiritual assistance is a supreme act of charity. Because "no believer should die in loneliness and

---

[82] John Paul II, Encyclical Letter *Evangelium vitae* (25th March 1995), 73: *AAS* 87 (1995), 486.

neglect",[83] it encompasses the patient with the solid support of human, and humanising, relationships to accompany them and open them to hope.

The parable of the Good Samaritan shows what the relationship with the suffering neighbour should be, what qualities should be avoided – indifference, apathy, bias, fear of soiling one's hands, totally occupied with one's own affairs – and what qualities should be embraced – attention, listening, understanding, compassion, and discretion.

The invitation to imitate the Samaritan's example— "Go and do likewise" (*Lk* 10:37)—is an admonition not to underestimate the full human potential of presence, of availability, of welcoming, of discernment, and of involvement, which nearness to one in need demands and which is essential to the integral care of the sick.

The quality of love and care for persons in critical and terminal stages of life contributes to assuaging the terrible, desperate desire to end one's life. Only human warmth and evangelical fraternity can reveal a positive horizon of support to the sick person in hope and confident trust.

Such accompaniment is part of the path defined by palliative care that includes the patients and their families.

The family has always played an important role in care, because their presence sustains the patient, and their love represents an essential therapeutic factor in the care of the sick person. Indeed, recalls Pope Francis, the family "has always been the nearest 'hospital' still today, in so many parts of the world, a hospital is for the privileged few, and is often far away. It is the mother, the father, brother, sisters and godparents who guarantee care and help one to heal".[84]

---

[83] Benedict XVI, *Address to the participants in the Congress organised by the Pontifical Academy for Life on the theme "Close by the incurable sick person and the dying: scientific and ethical aspects"* (25th February 2008): *AAS* 100 (2008), 171.

[84] Francis, *General Audience*, (10th June 2015): L'Osservatore Romano, 11th June 2015, 8.

Taking care of others, or providing care for the suffering of others, is a commitment that embraces not just a few but the entire Christian community. Saint Paul affirms that when one member suffers, it is the whole body that suffers (cf. *1 Cor* 12:26) and all bend to the sick to bring them relief. Everyone, for his or her part, is called to be a "servant of consolation" in the face of any human situation of desolation or discomfort.

Pastoral accompaniment involves the exercise of the human and Christian virtues of *empathy* (*en-pathos*), of *compassion* (*cum-passio*), of bearing another's suffering by sharing it, and of the *consolation* (*cum-solacium*), of entering into the solitude of others to make them feel loved, accepted, accompanied and sustained.

The ministry of listening and of consolation that the priest is called to offer, which symbolises the compassionate solicitude of Christ and the Church, can and must have a decisive role. In this essential mission it is extremely important to bear witness to and unite with that truth and charity with which the gaze of the Good Shepherd never ceases to accompany all of his children. Given the centrality of the priest in the pastoral, human and spiritual accompaniment of the sick at life's end, it is necessary that his priestly formation provide an updated and precise preparation in this area. It is also important that priests be formed in this Christian accompaniment. Since there may be particular circumstances that make it difficult for a priest to be present at the bedside, physicians and healthcare workers need this formation as well.

Being men and women skilled in humanity means that our way of caring for our suffering neighbour should favour their encounter with the Lord of life, who is the only one who can pour, in an efficacious manner, the oil of consolation and the wine of hope onto human wounds.

Every person has the natural right to be cared for, which at this time is the highest expression of the religion that one professes.

The sacramental moment is always the culmination of the entire pastoral commitment to care that precedes and is the source of all that follows.

The Church calls Penance and the Anointing of the Sick sacraments "of healing"[85], for they culminate in the Eucharist which is the "viaticum" for eternal life.[86] Through the closeness of the Church, the sick person experiences the nearness of Christ who accompanies them on their journey to their Father's house (cf. *Jn* 14:6) and helps the sick to not fall into despair,[87] by supporting them in hope especially when the journey becomes exhausting.[88]

11. PASTORAL DISCERNMENT TOWARDS THOSE WHO REQUEST EUTHANASIA OR ASSISTED SUICIDE

The pastoral accompaniment of those who expressly ask for euthanasia or assisted suicide today presents a singular moment when a reaffirmation of the teaching of the Church is necessary. With respect to the Sacrament of Penance and Reconciliation, the confessor must be assured of the presence of the true contrition *necessary for the validity of absolution* which consists in "sorrow of mind and a detestation for sin committed, with the purpose of not sinning for the future".[89] In this situation, we find ourselves before a person who, whatever their subjective dispositions may be, has decided upon a gravely immoral act and willingly persists in this decision. Such a state involves a manifest absence of the proper disposition for the reception of the

---

[85] *Catechism of the Catholic Church*, 1420.

[86] Cf. *Rituale Romanum, ex decreto Sacrosancti Oecumenici Concilii Vaticani II instauratum auctoritate Pauli PP. VI promulgatum, Ordo unctionis infirmorum eorumque pastoralis curae, Editio typica, Praenotanda*, Typis Polyglottis Vaticanis, Civitate Vaticana 1972, n. 26; *Catechism of the Catholic Church*, 1524.

[87] Cf. Francis, Encyclical Letter *Laudato si'* (24th May 2015), 235: *AAS* 107 (2015), 939.

[88] Cf. John Paul II, Encyclical Letter *Evangelium vitae* (25th March 1995), 67: *AAS* 87 (1995), 478-479.

[89] Council of Trent, Sess. XIV, *De sacramento penitentiae*, chap. 4: *DH* 1676.

Sacraments of Penance, with absolution,[90] and Anointing,[91] with Viaticum.[92] Such a penitent can receive these sacraments only when the minister discerns his or her readiness to take concrete steps that indicate he or she has modified their decision in this regard. Thus a person who may be registered in an association to receive euthanasia or assisted suicide must manifest the intention of cancelling such a registration before receiving the sacraments. It must be recalled that the necessity to postpone absolution does not imply a judgement on the imputability of guilt, since personal responsibility could be diminished or non-existent.[93] The priest could administer the sacraments to an unconscious person *sub condicione* if, on the basis of some signal given by the patient beforehand, he can presume his or her repentance.

The position of the Church here does not imply a non-acceptance of the sick person. It must be accompanied by a willingness to listen and to help, together with a deeper explanation of the nature of the sacrament, in order to provide the opportunity to desire and choose the sacrament up to the last moment. The Church is careful to look deeply for adequate signs of conversion, so that the faithful can reasonably ask for the reception of the sacraments. To delay absolution is a medicinal act of the Church, intended not to condemn, but to lead the sinner to conversion.

It is necessary to remain close to a person who may not be in the objective condition to receive the sacraments, for this nearness is an invitation to conversion, especially when euthanasia, requested or accepted, will not take place immediately or imminently. Here it remains possible to accompany the person whose hope may

---

[90] Cf. *Code of Canon Law*, can. 987.

[91] Cf. *Code of Canon Law*, can. 1007: "The anointing of the sick is not to be conferred upon those who persevere obstinately in manifest grave sin".

[92] Cf. *Code of Canon Law*, can. 915 and can. 843 § 1.

[93] Cf. Congregation for the Doctrine of the Faith, Declaration *Iura et bona*, II: *AAS* 72 (1980), 546.

be revived and whose erroneous decision may be modified, thus opening the way to admission to the sacraments.

Nevertheless, those who spiritually assist these persons should avoid any gesture, such as remaining until the euthanasia is performed, that could be interpreted as approval of this action. Such a presence could imply complicity in this act. This principle applies in a particular way, but is not limited to, chaplains in the healthcare systems where euthanasia is practised, for they must not give scandal by behaving in a manner that makes them complicit in the termination of human life.

12. THE REFORM OF THE EDUCATION AND FORMATION OF THE HEALTHCARE WORKERS

In today's social and cultural context, with so many challenges to the protection of human life in its most critical stages, education has a critical role to play. Families, schools, other educational institutions and parochial communities must work with determination to awaken and refine that sensitivity toward our neighbour and their suffering manifested by the Good Samaritan of the Gospel. [94]

Hospital chaplains should intensify the spiritual and moral formation of the healthcare workers, including physicians and nursing staff, as well as hospital volunteers, in order to prepare them to provide the human and psychological assistance necessary in the terminal stages of life. The psychological and spiritual care of patients and their families during the whole course of the illness must be a priority for the pastoral and healthcare workers.

Palliative treatments must be disseminated throughout the world. To this end, it would be desirable to organise academic courses of study for the specialised formation of healthcare workers. Also a priority is the dissemination of accurate general

---

[94] Cf. John Paul II, Apostolic Letter *Salvifici doloris* (11th February 1984), 29: *AAS* 76 (1984), 244-246.

information on the value of effective palliative treatments for a dignified accompaniment of the person until a natural death. Christian-inspired healthcare institutions should arrange for guidelines for the healthcare workers that include suitable methods for providing psychological, moral, and spiritual assistance as essential components of palliative care.

Human and spiritual assistance must again factor into academic formation of all healthcare workers as well as in hospital training programmes.

In addition, healthcare and assistance organisations must arrange for models of psychological and spiritual aid to healthcare workers who care for the terminally ill. *To show care for those who care* is essential so that healthcare workers and physicians do not bear all of the weight of the suffering and of the death of incurable patients (which can result in *burn out* for them). They need support and therapeutic sessions to process not only their values and feelings, but also the anguish they experience as they confront suffering and death in the context of their service to life. They need a profound sense of hope, along with the awareness that their own mission is a true vocation to accompany the mystery of life and grace in the painful and terminal stages of existence. [95]

---

[95] Cf. Francis, *Address to the doctors in Spain and Latin America: compassion is the very soul of medicine* (9th June 2016): *AAS* 108 (2016), 727-728. "Frailty, pain and infirmity are a difficult trial for everyone, including medical staff; they call for patience, for suffering-with; therefore, we must not give in to the functionalist temptation to apply rapid and drastic solutions moved by false compassion or by mere criteria of efficiency or cost-effectiveness. The dignity of human life is at stake; the dignity of the medical vocation is at stake".

CONCLUSION

The mystery of the Redemption of the human person is in an astonishing way rooted in the loving involvement of God with human suffering. That is why we can entrust ourselves to God and to convey this certainty in faith to the person who is suffering and fearful of pain and death.

Christian witness demonstrates that hope is always possible, even within a "throwaway culture". "The eloquence of the parable of the Good Samaritan and of the whole Gospel is especially this: every individual must feel as if *called personally* to bear witness to love in suffering".[96]

The Church learns from the Good Samaritan how to care for the terminally ill, and likewise obeys the commandment linked to the gift of life: "*respect, defend, love and serve life, every human life!*".[97] The gospel of life is a gospel of compassion and mercy directed to actual persons, weak and sinful, to relieve their suffering, to support them in the life of grace, and if possible to heal them from their wounds.

It is not enough, however, to share their pain; one needs to immerse oneself in the fruits of the Paschal Mystery of Christ who conquers sin and death, with the will "to dispel the misery of another, as if it were his own".[98] The greatest misery consists in the loss of hope in the face of death. This hope is proclaimed by the Christian witness, which, to be effective, must be lived in faith and encompass everyone — families, nurses, and physicians. It must engage the pastoral resources of the diocese and of Catholic healthcare centres, which are called to live with faith *the duty to accompany* the sick in all of the stages of illness, and in particular in the critical and terminal stages of life as defined in this letter.

---

[96] John Paul II, Apostolic Letter *Salvifici doloris* (11th February 1984), 29: *AAS* 76 (1984), 246.

[97] John Paul II, Encyclical Letter *Evangelium vitae* (25th March 1995), 5: *AAS* 87 (1995), 407.

[98] Saint Thomas Aquinas, *Summa Theologiae*, I, q. 21, a. 3.

The Good Samaritan, who puts the face of his brother in difficulty at the centre of his heart, and sees his need, offers him whatever is required to repair his wound of desolation and to open his heart to the luminous beams of hope.

The Samaritan's "willing the good" draws him near to the injured man not just with words or conversation, but with concrete actions and in truth (cf. *1 Jn* 3:18). It takes the form of care in the example of Christ who went about doing good and healing all (cf. *Acts* 10:38).

Healed by Jesus, we become men and women called to proclaim his healing power to love and provide the care for our neighbours to which he bore witness.

That the vocation to the love and care of another[99] brings with it the rewards of eternity is made explicit by the Lord of life in the parable of the final judgement: inherit the kingdom, for I was sick and you visited me. When did we do this, Lord? Every time you did it for the least ones, for a suffering brother or sister, you did it for me (cf. *Mt* 25:31-46).

The Sovereign Pontiff Francis, on 25th June 2020, approved the present Letter, adopted in the Plenary Session of this Congregation, the 29th of January 2020, and ordered its publication.

Rome, from the Offices of the Congregation for the Doctrine of the Faith, the 14th of July 2020, liturgical memorial of Saint Camillus de Lellis.

Luis F. Card. LADARIA, S.J.
Prefect

✠ Giacomo MORANDI
Titular Archbishop of Cerveteri
Secretary

---

[99] Cf. Benedict XVI, Encyclical Letter *Spe salvi* (30th November 2007), 39: *AAS* 99 (2007), 1016. "To suffer with the other and for others; to suffer for the sake of truth and justice; to suffer out of love and in order to become a person who truly loves – these are fundamental elements of humanity, and to abandon them would destroy man himself".